YP
784.09   Krischef
           The New Breed

1222
550

DATE DUE			

 Country Music Library

The NEW BREED

ROBERT K. KRISHEF

Lerner Publications Company ▪ Minneapolis

ACKNOWLEDGMENTS: The illustrations are reproduced through the courtesy of: pp. 4, 14, Country Music Foundation; p. 8, Capitol Records; pp. 16, 36, 41, 50, 54, RCA; p. 22, Top Billing; pp. 28, 32, 34, Warner Brothers Records; p. 58, Mercury Records; pp. 64, 69, Janice Smith and the Academy of Country Music.

Front cover photo: Warner Brothers Records

Imperial Public Library
Imperial, Texas

LIBRARY OF CONGRESS CATALOGING IN PUBLICATION DATA

Krishef, Robert K.
The new breed.

(Country Music Library)
Includes index.
SUMMARY: Biographies of nine contemporary country music stars, including Glen Campbell, John Denver, Emmylou Harris, and Dolly Parton.

1. Country musicians — United States — Biography — Juvenile literature. [1. Musicians. 2. Country music.] I. Title.

ML3930.A2K74   784'.092'2 [B] [920]   77-90153
ISBN 0-8225-1406-0

Copyright © 1978 by Lerner Publications Company

All rights reserved. International copyright secured. No part of this book may be reproduced in any form whatsoever without permission in writing from the publisher except for the inclusion of brief quotations in an acknowledged review.

Manufactured in the United States of America. Published simultaneously in Canada by J. M. Dent & Sons (Canada) Ltd., Don Mills, Ontario.

International Standard Book Number: 0-8225-1406-0
Library of Congress Catalog Card Number: 77-90153

1 2 3 4 5 6 7 8 9 10 85 84 83 82 81 80 79 78

Contents

	Introduction	5
1	Glen Campbell	9
2	John Denver	17
3	Tom T. Hall	23
4	Emmylou Harris	29
5	Waylon Jennings	37
6	Ronnie Milsap	45
7	Dolly Parton	51
8	Johnny Rodriguez	59
9	Tanya Tucker	65
	Index	72

Johnny Rodriguez, one of the "new breed"

Introduction

Country music, like other forms of creative expression, is in a constant state of change. In the 19th and early 20th centuries, this kind of music was popular mainly in the rural areas of the southern United States. Very few people in the big cities then knew or appreciated the "pickin' and singin'" that went on in barn dances and theaters throughout the South. But with the advent of the recording industry and radio, country music began to capture nationwide attention. Today even large metropolitan areas such as New York have full-time country radio stations.

Much of the country music that is now popular nationwide is far different from old-style country music, however. Country music now tends to emphasize voices rather than instruments. Even some of the instruments themselves have changed.

When once the fiddle was heard above all the noise at a barn dance, now the heavy beat of an electric guitar dominates the country music of radio and television.

There have been other significant changes in the field of country music, too. With network television, a huge recording industry, and thousands of radio stations playing country songs, the newest generation of singers has a better chance than ever of becoming well-known. And this marks the main difference between today's young singers and those of, say, 40 years ago. While early country music performers had to struggle for years to become known outside the South, today's singers and instrumentalists come from anywhere, and can be introduced throughout the country over television in a matter of seconds. As a result, today's performers influence the tastes of millions of fans more quickly than ever. The fans, in turn, influence singers by making instant "hits" out of their favorite tunes.

Many of the performers who currently dominate the country scene look, act, sing, and think differently than those who came before them. This new breed consists of performers who have broken with tradition. They sometimes have a lot more hair than their predecessors, and some of them come from backgrounds that are anything but rural and southern. Sometimes the music they perform mixes the sounds of pop and rock with the traditional country sounds. The new breed also consists of many women superstars, unlike the old-style singing stars, who were usually men.

The major new breed figures—among them Glen Campbell, John Denver, Tom T. Hall, Emmylou Harris, Waylon Jennings, Ronnie Milsap, Dolly Parton, Johnny Rodriguez, and Tanya Tucker—are products of today's modern and industrial society. These performers are representative of today's tastes and today's people. In another 40 years, some of these stars will have faded from public memory. But perhaps some will become a permanent part of country music history, like many of yesterday's heroes and heroines.

The music fans of the future may look back on some members of today's new breed and sigh. They may think then that "songs aren't being written or sung the way they used to be." But this nostalgia and sentimentality is only natural. It is a sign of health and growth in country music, which gives rise to each new generation of singers and to the changes they bring. As long as country music makes way for change, there will always be a new breed.

Glen Campbell 1

The age of television created exciting new opportunities for performers. By winning the favor of vast TV audiences, young unknowns could achieve almost immediate wealth and fame. The opportunity to appear on nationwide television reached country music show people in the late 1960s, when the networks began featuring their kind of music. One of the first country performers to reach stardom through television was Glen Campbell, a grinning, round-faced guitar player with straw-colored hair and a pleasant voice.

Campbell wasn't exactly starving before he became a star. In fact, he was earning between $75,000 and $100,000 a year as a leading studio musician in Los Angeles, playing at recording sessions. He backed such artists as Frank Sinatra, Dean Martin, Elvis Presley, the Beach Boys, Merle Haggard, and Buck Owens. Glen also was known for two hits of his own, "Gentle on My Mind" and "By the Time I Get to Phoenix." The first song won Glen a Grammy award from the National Academy of Recording Arts and Sciences for "best country solo" in 1967. The second song got him a Grammy for "best contemporary solo."

Because of these two songs, Campbell was influential in creating a new category, a modern country pop sound. This was the sound Glen made popular nationwide when he became a summer replacement for the Smothers Brothers television show in 1968. The show led to his own TV program, "The Glen Campbell Goodtime Hour."

The Campbell program opened the eyes and ears of millions of viewers to the fact that country music did not have to be "corny." "We're not shuckin' it right off the cob anymore," Campbell said of his music. "There can be more to the music than a fiddle, a banjo, and a rhythm guitar. The new country sound is much smoother." In speaking of the new sound, Glen is always quick to add that he respects the more traditional country singers. Such singers, he says, added much to the country music sound and were "great in their time. But this isn't their time."

Despite his sophisticated new sound, Campbell is still a "country boy." Part of his appeal on television lies in his wholesome looks, his naturalness, and his "down-home" way of talking. "Wooowheee!" he shouted on one of his shows. "Ah been busier than a three-headed woodpecker!" Glen Campbell has always sounded exactly like what he is: an ex-cotton picker from the Ozarks.

Born April 22, 1936, Glen was the seventh of twelve children. Young Campbell grew up in Delight, Arkansas—population 450—sharing a bed with three brothers, working in the cotton fields, and helping to care for the cows, pigs, and chickens. Most of the farm work was done by hand. The Campbells didn't even have a tractor for plowing, and Glen recalls spending much of his early life "looking at the north end of a south-bound mule."

Life was not all work for young Campbell, though. When he was four years old, Glen's father bought him a five-dollar guitar out of a Sears and Roebuck catalog. His father and an uncle taught Glen a few chords, and the boy soon learned to play songs simply by listening to the radio. By the time Glen was six, people could tell that he had unusual talent for one so young. He soon began playing part-time with a western band led by another uncle, Dick Bills.

Bills later moved to Albuquerque, New Mexico, but this didn't put an end to Campbell's career. Glen continued performing around home until he was in his middle teens. Then he left school and took odd jobs in Texas and Wyoming. In the early 1950s, Glen rejoined the Bills group in New

Mexico. The group had a radio show, a regular nightclub act, and numerous bookings at rodeos, high school proms, picnics, and other events.

Campbell by then had become a featured performer with the band. But he was already developing musical tastes that were too modern for his uncle, so he left the group in 1958 to form his own band. One night, while playing with his new band at a club in Albuquerque, Glen met Billie Nunely, the girl whom he would marry a year later.

After the wedding in 1959, the young couple decided that their future lay in California, where Glen had been invited to join a band. With fairytale stars in their eyes, they loaded their belongings into a small trailer hitched to their 1957 Chevrolet and headed for what they believed to be the promised land. Their total savings was $300. Campbell didn't get his job, however, so Billie worked in a bank while Glen auditioned at various recording studios and companies. He soon found full-time work and also played part-time with several rock bands in the Los Angeles area.

It wasn't long before Glen was in demand at the recording studios. Many artists and music arrangers wanted him because he was so versatile —he could play 12-string and 6-string guitar, 5-string banjo, mandolin, and bass. And his voice blended well in background harmony. Glen was such a good musician that one year he played at more than 580 recording sessions. Some of the song arrangers in the studios were fascinated by the skill of the country boy who they knew was basically self-taught. When they asked him if he could read music, he grinned, "Not enough to hurt my pickin', man." Actually, Campbell could not—and does not now—read a note of music.

With all his singing experience, Glen's voice improved steadily, and he began getting a reputation for his ability as a vocalist as well as a "picker."

The young "picker" from Arkansas

From right to left: *Glen Campbell, Tammy Wynette, Sheb Wooley, Dolly Parton, and Porter Wagoner at the Country Music Association's awards show in 1968*

He made some records that were modest hits in the early and middle 1960s, including "Turn Around, Look at Me" and "Too Late to Worry, Too Blue to Cry." But he didn't really find the singing sound he wanted until he discovered the song "Gentle on My Mind," written by Nashville's John Hartford. This song has since become Glen Campbell's trademark.

Campbell's fame spread so fast that in 1968 he was named "Entertainer of the Year" by the Country Music Association. In 1969, he won numerous awards from the Academy of Country Music, the Music Operators of America, and trade magazines such as *Record World, Cash Box,* and *Billboard.* He had follow-up record hits, among them "Wichita Lineman" and "Galveston." And he also won leading roles in the movies *True Grit* (with John Wayne) and *Norwood.*

Campbell's "Goodtime Hour" went off the air after four years on television. But his career and the country pop sound he nurtured are far from over. Glen is still a popular nightclub attraction in Las Vegas, New York, and other cities. He also appears as a guest on various television shows. And, after a temporary lull in his recording career, he has bounced back with the hit "Rhinestone Cowboy." His personal life, like his professional life, has had its ups and downs. He was divorced from his wife, Billie, and is now remarried.

Occasionally Campbell gets upset with the tumult and gossip of the show business world. He longs for the peace and quiet of the Ozarks. Still, from the time his father put a guitar in his hand, Glen Campbell was destined to be a performer. It is hard to imagine country pop without him.

John Denver 2

"What in the world is country music coming to," complained a long-time fan, "when John Denver can be the Country Music Association Entertainer of the Year!"

This complaint continues to be voiced by some country music fans, not because Denver is a bad singer but because he is really not a country singer. He is instead a pop singer, a soft rock singer, and a folksinger. John is so versatile, however, that he is able to "become" a country singer at will, adapting certain country sounds and ideas into his material.

This "crossing over" can be hard for a traditional country fan to take. Yet there is no doubt that many people who enjoy country music also like to listen to Denver and buy his records. He sells millions of records to a variety of fans, draws sellout crowds for concerts, and attracts huge viewing audiences for his television specials. The reason he appeals to country folks as well as to other fans is that some of his songs have a country flavor to their lyrics or musical arrangements. For example, one of his songs is about "country roads," while "Thank God I'm a Country Boy" is arranged very much like a barn-dance hoedown.

Denver shares another common ground with traditional country singers. Like all good country artists, John seeks to communicate with his audience. He sings songs that tell a story and make people think—a story and a message have always been important to country fans. And his themes, such as the desire to "come back home," are often simple and touching.

For Denver, home is an especially heartfelt subject for songs. His own home life was often unsettled as he was growing up, because his family was always moving. Born Henry John Deutschendorf, Jr., on December 31, 1943, in New Mexico, John spent his childhood years in several different places. Because his father was a career officer in the Air Force, John and his family lived in New Mexico, California, Ohio, Japan, Arizona, Alabama, and Texas. Making friends under such circumstances was rather difficult. "I always was kind of lonely," says Denver..

As a result of all this moving, John might have become shy and withdrawn had it not been for music. When he was 13, his grandmother gave him an old 1910 Gibson guitar that she had used many years before. John enjoyed learning to play the guitar. But he wasn't really interested in it until he realized that music was a way for him to meet people. He was thrilled the first time he played in front of a group of students and was applauded. After that, he carried his guitar around nearly everywhere he went, hoping that people would ask him to play.

By the time John entered high school, he was part of a band that was in demand at parties. He was living in Texas at the time, a period that turned out to be relatively happy and secure for him. But like many other young people, he didn't know what he wanted to do with his life. Since his eyesight wasn't good enough for the Air Force, he couldn't fulfill his dream of becoming an Air Force pilot like his dad. Although music was enjoyable for John, his parents did not see much future in it. They wanted their son to go to college, so, without any great enthusiasm, he agreed to enroll at Texas Tech.

There John studied architecture for nearly three years. But it was clear almost from the start that he was doing the wrong thing in the wrong place. His most satisfying times at Texas Tech were when he was performing with a rhythm and blues band and soloing. Eventually he began devoting more time to music than to his studies. Finally he mustered enough courage to quit school and jump into show business.

In 1963 John headed for California in his 10-year-old Chevrolet, loaded with everything he owned. He had $125 and no job prospects. "But I was happier than I had ever been in my life," he says, recalling those days. There he found work as an architectural draftsman during the day and as a singer in coffeehouses at night. Soon he managed to make enough money as a singer to quit his draftsman's job.

In 1965, John auditioned for a spot with the Chad Mitchell Trio, then one of the leading folk groups in the country. He replaced Chad Mitchell, who had left to do a solo act. Gradually John emerged as the lead tenor of the trio. Audiences liked his spirited, warm voice, especially when he sang "Leaving on a Jet Plane." It was his own composition, one that he had written for the folk group Peter, Paul, and Mary.

Life unfolded quickly for Henry John Deutschendorf in the middle and late 1960s. On a concert tour of Minnesota in 1966, he fell in love with a college student, Annie Martell. They were married the following year. Meanwhile the trio was breaking up, because folk groups were no longer very popular.

By that time John was ready to try show business as a solo artist again. He decided that he needed a shortened name and chose "Denver," simply because he liked the Colorado area. In fact, he and

Annie eventually settled in Colorado. While the "new John Denver" was looking for more recording material and singing engagements, "Leaving on a Jet Plane" was released as a single by Peter, Paul, and Mary. It became one of the smash hits of 1969, thus helping Denver financially and giving him even more prestige in the music world. RCA awarded him a recording contract, partly because his "Jet Plane" song was such a success.

Denver has always regarded himself primarily as an entertainer rather than a songwriter. It is a combination of both talents, though, that has put him on top. John's success is still spiraling upward. A song that he wrote with folk singers Bill Danoff and Taffy Nivert became a classic among contemporary pop and country tunes of the early 1970s— it was "Take Me Home, Country Roads." This Denver hit was soon followed by "Rocky Mountain High," "Follow Me," and "Goodbye Again."

Country Music Association members took official note of John's popularity in 1975 by awarding him the "top entertainer" award. He also received the songwriter award that year for his single "Back Home Again." He was among the top five finalists for "Male Vocalist of the Year," "Best Single Record" ("Thank God I'm a Country Boy"), and "Best Album" ("An Evening with John Denver"). It wasn't a bad night for someone who wasn't even a country singer.

Tom T. Hall 3

For a long time, members of the country music establishment were nervous about songwriter and performer Tom T. Hall. After all, he was a well-read man who had been to college—not much like most country music performers. And he was a liberal who had supported George McGovern for the presidency in 1972. Not only that, but he was also friendly with the "renegades" of country music—the anti-establishment people such as Waylon Jennings, Kris Kristofferson, and Willie Nelson. And Tom T. even liked the movie *Nashville*, which many people in Nashville considered a devastating put-down of country music.

In an industry that is growing ever more conscious of its image, an outspoken person such as Hall can make many people uncomfortable. Yet Hall in his own way is as concerned with the image of country music as anyone else. His songs, which have messages that are meaningful to nearly everyone, have helped make country music acceptable even to city folks. And he has done this by being more of a "country boy" than many of the Nashville "establishment" people who are upset by his independent, sometimes rebellious attitudes.

Traditionally country music has been a storytelling kind of music that places more importance on the words than on the music. Hall grew up listening to such music in Olive Hill, Kentucky, where he was born May 25, 1936. Recalling his boyhood, he says that he can't remember a time when he didn't want to be in show business. As a teenager, he had his own band, called the "Kentucky Travelers." And he became a disc jockey before joining the army in 1957.

It was while he was in the army that Hall decided he wanted to become a writer. He wasn't sure what kind of writing suited him, although he knew he liked to write songs. After his discharge from the army, Tom drifted around for a while, but then decided to reorganize his band. He also took disc jockey jobs and enrolled in journalism classes at Roanoke College in Salem, Virginia.

Gradually Hall concentrated more on songwriting than on any other kind of writing. He sent his songs away to several publishers, and soon a Nashville publishing company, Newkeys Music, bought his material. His first song to be published and recorded, "D.J. for a Day," became a hit. Hall signed a contract with Newkeys and worked with that company for eight years before forming his own publishing company, Hallnote Music.

By the mid-1960s, Nashville executives were pressuring Tom to make records himself, but he resisted the idea. "I guess I believed in singleness of purpose at the time," he said. "When people would come to me with a recording contract, I'd say, 'Listen, I don't want to whistle, sing, or dance. I want to write.'" And write he did, with a special ability to tell stories in the best country music tradition.

Hall's songs are inspired by seemingly simple everyday ideas. He wants his songs to have feeling and simplicity so that listeners can say, "And I thought I was the only person who felt that way." For instance, his song "Who's Going to Feed the Hogs?" is about a real-life farmer whom Tom met in the hospital. In the song, the farmer shows greater concern about his hogs than about himself. But the lyrics could have been about anyone worrying about the uncertainties of life.

Many of Tom's ideas for songs come from conversations with strangers. For example, a trucker once asked Tom to autograph a record to "Ravishing Ruby," a name Tom later used in one of his truck-stop songs. And an old janitor once sat down with Tom to discuss "old dogs, children, and watermelon wine," which inspired Hall to write a song of the same name.

Like many writers, Hall writes about what he knows. He tells about a woman in his hometown who was criticized by the townspeople for her wild way of living. The woman's child was spanked regularly at school, because the teachers assumed that such a child could not be getting proper discipline at home. One day the child's mother walked into a PTA meeting and told everyone off—she said that the members were not practicing what they preached. The tune that was born from this incident was "Harper Valley PTA," released in 1968. Until then, Tom T. was a reasonably successful songwriter, living on royalties of $15,000 to $20,000 a year. But after this song, he became one of the best known writers in the music business. "Harper Valley PTA" sold more than two million copies that year and so far has earned Hall about one million dollars. The song also made a celebrity out of Jeannie C. Riley, the artist who recorded it.

At that time, Hall changed his mind about limiting himself to writing. He decided that if his songs were going to become popular, he might as well be the one to record them. He soon signed a contract with Mercury Records and subsequently recorded "Ballad of Forty Dollars," "Salute to a Switchblade," "A Week in a Country Jail," "I Love," "Country Is," and "Sneaky Snake," all of which became hits. One of the best sellers, a favorite of his, was "The Year that Clayton Delaney Died." It was a true story about a guitar picker who was such a hero to Hall that he went off in the woods and cried when the old musician died.

Besides writing, recording, and publishing, Tom T. keeps busy with concert tours. He performs before audiences across the nation—from New York's Madison Square Garden to South Dakota's state fair. He also appears on television variety and talk shows, and on national TV commercials. Because of the commercials, more people than ever now recognize the stocky man with the deep voice.

Hall accepts his fame with mixed feelings. He used to be able to roam the country, looking for new song material without people feeling as though they knew him from somewhere. But now that he is well known, "just plain folks" don't talk to him as freely anymore. He believes that fame and success are destroying his freedom to record the story of the common man and woman.

There is no doubt that Hall will continue to write, though. He has too much to say, and his brand of frankness—some call it "musical journalism"—has made country music meaningful for everyone. "Tom T. Hall," reported *Rolling Stone Magazine,* "says as much as anyone currently putting voice to tape about this country, its people, and what is happening to it and to them."

Emmylou Harris 4

In 1963, when Emmylou Harris was 16 years old, folk music was just beginning to stir the imaginations of listeners in East Coast coffeehouses and on college campuses. Like the "restless wind" sung about in so many folk tunes, Emmylou was always on the move, searching for her own identity and a meaning to life. Unlike many of her friends, she was not satisfied with the traditional high school football games and beauty contests.

Emmylou's dissatisfaction continued to grow even after she entered the University of North Carolina on a drama scholarship in 1965. Her free spirit was not suited to college discipline, and she found studying and dormitory life too confining. Emmylou quit after her third semester and eventually wound up in Greenwich Village in New York, where she tried to launch a career in music.

"Unfortunately, it wasn't really the most opportune time to try to make it as a folk singer," she recalls with a soft smile. The once-growing interest in folk music had almost died, it seemed, while she was waiting on tables in college.

By the late 1960s and early '70s, Emmylou's life had reached a frustrating low. She felt trapped after signing a four-year recording contract that controlled the kinds of songs she could release. Besides that, she was in the middle of ending an unhappy marriage, to which a daughter had been born in 1970. As soon as Emmylou was divorced, she went to Maryland, where her parents lived, and put thoughts of a musical career behind her. "I had to be concerned about other things," she said, "such as earning a living for myself and my child."

At the urging of friends, Emmylou began singing in local clubs and bars in the Washington, D.C., area. Her friends knew that music would be good for her, and they were right. It soon became the most important thing in Emmylou's life again, even though she was earning as little as 5 or 10 dollars a night. The money, however, was far less important than the exposure that she was getting—Emmylou was in the limelight once more.

After entertaining at different clubs for about a year, Emmylou settled down to play the Cellar Door, a club in Washington, D.C. Members of the band called the "Flying Burrito Brothers" were in the audience one night. They were so impressed by her singing that they immediately asked her to join them. With visions of stardom in her eyes, Emmylou eagerly accepted. One week later, however, she was crushed to learn that the Burrito Brothers were breaking up their act. Her first and last concert with them took place in nearby Baltimore. In the audience was singer-guitarist Gram Parsons.

Like other performers of the early 1970s, Parsons was trying to develop a bold new sound out of simple, nostalgic country music and heavy, thudding rock-and-roll. The difference between Parsons and other performers, however, was that he was succeeding at blending the two sounds. Impressed with Emmylou's folk and rock styles, he invited her to sing with him when he made his new album, "GP."

"Every few months," Emmylou said, "he'd call me and say he was almost ready to begin recording." But after each call, nothing would happen. Emmylou started telling herself that it all had been too good to be true. "Then one day, I got a ticket to Los Angeles in the mail," she said. "I went, and we did the album."

Although Emmylou had grown up with country music, she had never paid much attention to it. In spite of the fact that she had been born and raised in the South and had taught herself to play the guitar by listening to country tunes, Emmylou had always been more comfortable with folk music. Oddly enough, it was Parsons who finally turned her on to the country sound. Parsons helped make her aware of the great feeling shown by such country singers as George Jones and the Louvin brothers. With Parsons, Emmylou heard the real sounds of country music for the first time. A new world opened up for her.

In the spring of 1973 after the "GP" album had been recorded, Emmylou went on tour with

Emmylou singing in a coffeehouse

Parsons and worked with him on another album, "Grievous Angel." That summer, at the age of 26, Parsons suffered a heart attack and died. Emmylou was so stunned by the loss of her personal friend and teacher that she could not bear the thought of returning to California without him. Instead, she went back to the area around Washington, D.C., and began working in small clubs again. Her career once more came to a standstill.

Emmylou's nightclub work lasted only a short while, however. Warner Brothers Record executives liked her performance on the Parsons albums so much that they gave her a recording contract in mid-1974. Early in 1975, Warner Brothers released a new Harris album "Pieces of the Sky," produced by Brian Ahern, also a producer for singer Anne Murray. The musicians for the album, Ronnie Tutt, James Burton, and Glen D. Hardin, were from Elvis Presley's band. With such talented assistants backing Emmylou's warm, emotional voice, the album became one of the country hits of the year. One of the album's songs, "If I Could Only Win Your Love," was also released as a single that reached the top of country music charts.

Emmylou's career continued to climb. In 1976, she recorded with Bob Dylan on his album "Desire" and had her own hit album, "Elite Hotel." This album included such material as "Together Again" by Buck Owens, "Here, There, and Every-

Emmylou Harris, a leading singer of "country rock"

where" by the Beatles, "Jambalaya" by Hank Williams, and "Sin City" and "Wheels" by Gram Parsons. The album and two singles by Harris were nominated for awards by the Country Music Association. And Emmylou was one of the five finalists for the association's "Female Vocalist of the Year" award.

Today Emmylou Harris is one of the leading women singers of the new sound that blends country and hard rock—"country rock," as it is called by some people. Even though she is one of the new breed, Emmylou sees herself simply as a country singer. Now that she is famous, her new status as a nationally known country artist still leaves her breathless and amazed. She continues to be surprised when people want her autograph. And she is especially flattered when other artists record her songs, as Dolly Parton did with "Boulder to Birmingham."

Only while performing is Emmylou able to shed the feeling that success is all a dream and that she soon must be moving on. Simply dressed, with long, flowing black hair, Emmylou is a star on stage. Her voice commands the attention of the audience. She is a soprano with the range and versatility to hit notes with strength as well as tenderness. She isn't sure how she does it. "I'm not a trained singer," she says. "I just sing what I feel." Clearly the restless teenager of the 1960s has found her roots in country music.

Waylon Jennings 5

Thousands of fans in the "Grand Ole Opry" audience and millions watching over television breathlessly awaited Tennessee Ernie Ford's announcement. They were about to find out who would become the Country Music Association's 1976 "Entertainer of the Year."

Four of the five nominees for the award were present that evening and had already entertained the audience. "The fifth nominee, Waylon Jennings, is unable to be here tonight," announced Ford in a strained, clipped voice. "But let's get on with it," he said as he opened the envelope containing the winner's name. With a broad grin, he announced that the winner was Mel Tillis.

There was a shout of joy and a burst of applause among the audience. It was a popular choice. Mel Tillis, an all-around veteran performer, richly deserved the honor. Along with the cheers, however, came a sigh of relief among the country music executives that Jennings had not won.

The "establishment" and Jennings have not gotten along very well, and Waylon further strained the relationship that year by asking to have his name withdrawn from consideration for "Entertainer of the Year." His request came too late, however. The votes had already been cast. To make matters worse, Jennings refused to show up for the awards that night—still another embarrassment to the community.

Even his friend and sometimes working partner Willie Nelson said he was a little disappointed that Jennings was not there, "although I respect his decision." Nelson, while he did not win the top honor either, was up on the stage three times that night to accept other awards "on behalf of me and old Waylon." The two were named "Vocal Duo of the Year," and they also won awards for the best single, "Good Hearted Woman," and the best album, "Wanted—The Outlaws." Jessi Colter, Waylon's wife, and Tompall Glaser also shared in the album victory.

The album title "Outlaws" referred to a certain group of rebellious country performers, of which Jennings is a part. Besides Jennings, there are Nelson, Glaser, Colter, Kris Kristofferson, Billy Jo Shaver, David Allan Coe, Kinky Friedman, and others. They are called "outlaws" or "renegades" of country music, because they are always bucking the system that produces most of the music. Waylon is generally considered the unofficial "king of the outlaws."

It is hard to pin down the reasons for Jenning's dislike of the system and the system's dislike of him. Some country music fans think that his music leans a little too heavily toward rock, but there is nothing unusual about "country rock" today. Although Jennings has grown a beard and allowed his hair to become long, that, too, is no longer unusual—performers in general are hairier nowadays. His anti-establishment attitudes can, perhaps, be seen more readily in his past experience with drugs. In the 1960s, Jennings had problems with pills and was living a rather self-destructive life. He and friend Johnny Cash were traveling down the same crash course; however, both pulled out in time.

Although Jennings has gone through many changes in his life, he still is considered an outlaw by country music folk. Perhaps the underlying reason for his rebellious nature lies in his personal philosophy. He is a free spirit, an individualist, and he does not want other people telling him what to record or how to record. His musical style is "strictly Waylon."

Yet Waylon insists that he is not trying to destroy the musical establishment. "For some, it's a good system," he says. Nor is he trying to hurt country music. "I am part of it, and I'll be the first to defend it." But he wants the right to say what he believes and to make his own changes in his music. He feels that the "bureaucrats on Nashville's Music Row," the executives who make the important production decisions, are unable (or unwilling) to put forth the effort required for real quality and creativity.

Of course, Jennings is not alone in his battle. He has supporters and sympathizers among fans, fellow performers, and even among executives on Music Row. The difference is that most of these people are still operating within the system. In spite of Jenning's squabbles with the system, the Country Music Association did vote him "Male Vocalist of the Year" in 1975. "And it's about time," said co-master of ceremonies Glen Campbell when the decision was announced.

Jennings, indeed deserves the title, for he is talented and has been in the business for a long time. He started young. Born June 15, 1937, in Littlefield, Texas, he began playing the guitar when he was 7 and became a hometown radio disc jockey at the age of 12. As the youngest disc jockey in the nation, he spent his teenage years spinning records and singing for audiences in Littlefield and surrounding towns.

In 1958, Jennings went to Lubbock, Texas, and continued working as a disc jockey until he met rock-and-roll star Buddy Holly. He soon joined Holly's band, the Crickets, as a bass guitarist and began touring with the group. In February 1959, the Crickets had a booking in Moorhead, Minnesota. Holly chartered a light plane to take some of the group to Moorhead, and Jennings was scheduled to go with him. At the last moment, though, another member of the band asked to take Waylon's place. A few hours after takeoff, the plane crashed and all the occupants were killed. Jennings was in

Waylon and the "establishment" do not get along very well.

a state of shock. He not only had come near to death himself, but he had also lost Holly, his close friend and professional advisor.

The tragedy temporarily drove Waylon away from onstage performing. He went back to Lubbock and started working in radio again. Then he moved to Phoenix, Arizona, where he formed his own band, the Waylors. The group played a combination of rock and country music in nightclubs around the Phoenix area. Soon they were headliners at "J.D.'s," one of Phoenix's top clubs.

"He was setting the town on fire," recalls his wife, Jessi, who met him at the club. "Cowboys would drive hundreds of miles to see him. Women would take all week getting dolled up to go to the club on Saturday night."

The word got back to Nashville about Waylon Jennings' popularity. Among country music executives who personally checked him out was Chet Atkins. He signed Jennings for RCA Records in 1965. Waylon has since made more than 20 albums for RCA, including "The Ramblin' Man," "This Time," "Dreaming My Dreams," "Lonesome, On'ry and Mean," and "Honky Tonk Heroes."

A variety of producers, among them Atkins, have worked with Jennings at his recording sessions. Unlike most country artists, Waylon has not been able to stick with one producer. He has now reached the conclusion that "basically I have to be my own producer. I have to have the last say."

When Jennings is not busy recording, he is making concert appearances. He has entertained thousands of people at open-air music festivals, in stadiums, at amusement parks, and in large auditoriums. He appears on both variety shows and talk shows, even though he gets upset with talk show hosts. He believes that they "talk down" to country performers. "To them, 'country' still has the hayseed image," he remarked. "But I know country people who are as smart or smarter than anyone."

Waylon Jennings, a country boy to the bone, is both smart and ambitious. He is moving up in the entertainment world. But the words that perhaps best describe him are those in the title of a movie he once made—"Nashville Rebel." He still insists upon having the last say.

Ronnie Milsap 6

One evening during a performance, Ronnie Milsap wandered too near the edge of the stage and fell off into the orchestra pit. He landed with a jolt. Shaken but unhurt, he got up immediately and was even able to joke about his fall. "That's the first time I ever saw stars," said young Milsap, who has been blind since birth.

There is no grimness or self-pity in such a remark, for Ronnie is not overly sensitive about his handicap. A positive person by nature, he doesn't really view himself as handicapped, except when it comes to driving a car or picking out clothes. In fact, Ronnie sees himself as a very lucky man in many respects—one of them being his success as a country singer.

There have been other blind entertainers in the history of country music, but none who have achieved Ronnie Milsap's prominence. Lemon

Jefferson and Riley Puckett were two such entertainers of the 1920s. Unlike Milsap, these sightless entertainers and others who followed were popular only as instrumentalists. More recently Ray Charles has attained popularity as a vocalist. However, while Charles sings some country tunes and has influenced many country singers, he is not really a country singer.

Ronnie Milsap is not only a singer and an instrumentalist, but he is also "pure country." His music throbs with a heavy "honky tonk" beat, aided by his own piano accompaniment. The sound is recognized as a good one, for Milsap was voted country "Male Vocalist of the Year" in 1974 by the National Academy of Recording Arts and Sciences and by the Country Music Association. In 1976 and 1977, he won the same award again from the Country Music Association, and was named "Country Artist of the Year" by *Billboard Magazine.*

These awards came to Ronnie only two years after he entered the country music business, making him one of the newest and brightest country stars. Few singers in country music have attained such success so quickly. Yet Milsap's success story is not as simple as it might seem. Like many other country music performers, Ronnie served a musical apprenticeship, but one far different from that of most of his peers. As a youngster, he was a serious student of classical music, becoming a rock musician in his teen years.

Ronnie Milsap was born in Robbinsville, North Carolina, a small farming community near the Tennessee border. There were no schools for blind people in Robbinsville, so in 1950, at the age of five, Ronnie was sent to the State School for the Blind in Raleigh, North Carolina. There his aptitude for music was discovered, and the school gave him the opportunity to develop his natural musical talents in a classical direction.

By the age of 7, Ronnie was a virtuoso on the violin. He also played the piano and became proficient on the guitar by the time he was 12. As a student, he enjoyed composers such as Mozart "for his melodies" and Bach "for his complicated techniques." Thanks to Ronnie's own talent and his early classical training, he now can play most of the keyboard instruments and also the strings, percussions, and woodwinds.

But classical music was not enough for Ronnie when he was in school. In spite of his grounding in the classics and his love for rock, Ronnie could not forget the country sound that had filled the first five years of his life. His musical ear and soul had been awakened by the hard-hitting, wailing sounds on radio and by the records of performers such as Hank Williams, Roy Acuff, Elvis Presley, Jerry Lee Lewis, and Lefty Frizzell. To the despair of Ronnie's teachers, he would take every opportunity to pound out forbidden tunes on the piano. He was suspended several times for his disobedience, but finally the school gave up and allowed him and three other blind boys to form a band. They called themselves the Apparitions and performed at high school and college assemblies around Raleigh and Chapel Hill.

After graduation from high school, Ronnie attended Young-Harris Junior College in Atlanta, Georgia. There he studied pre-law and was granted a scholarship to law school at Emory University in Atlanta. But Ronnie's love of music won out over a legal career. He rejected the scholarship, stayed in Atlanta, and began working as a sideman (a backup musician) for J.J. Cale and for other entertainers.

By 1966, Milsap had his own band and was playing the nightclub and college circuits. For six years, he experimented with different sorts of popular music—rock, jazz, and country. As his success grew, he began recording for Scepter Records, later for Chips Records, and then for Warner Brothers. Even though there was plenty of work for Ronnie, he began to feel a little dissatisfied. He had a feeling that all he was doing was earning a living for himself and his wife, Joyce, whom he had married when he was 19. Ronnie knew that something was missing, and finally he decided that the problem was with the rock music he was playing. "I have played, and can play, any kind of music," he said. "But you must do what your heart feels is right. And to me, that's country."

So Ronnie followed his heart and moved his wife and their infant son, Todd, to Nashville, Tennessee, the capital of country music. He became a part of the country music scene immediately. It was almost as if he were the final piece to a jigsaw puzzle. In January 1973, Ronnie got a job at the King of the Road nightclub in Nashville, which soon led to a major recording contract with RCA Records.

As Ronnie looks back on his career today, he feels that his earlier record releases were too slick —that they lacked sincerity. He considers his later releases "more honest for me. I believed in them," he said, "and they made me feel good." His sincerity, he believes, is what makes the listeners feel good, too. His feelings have come through in such hits as "(All Together Now) Let's Fall Apart," "The Girl that Waits on Tables," "Legend in My Time," "Pure Love," and "Please Don't Tell Me How the Story Ends," all of which were in the top five on national charts. The last two discs reached the number one position and helped make Ronnie an overnight success. Now Opry audiences, like millions of other fans, are applauding Ronnie Milsap's music and laughing with him as he jokes between numbers. He is a star who is as human as he is talented.

Dolly Parton 7

Since the 1920s, country music has been an up-and-coming industry. But in the first 40 years of the country music business, women were seldom featured as stars. Of course, there were women artists such as Maybell and Sara Carter who performed with groups. But there were few female solo artists.

This situation began to change after World War II, with the emergence of singers such as Rose Maddox, Molly O'Day, and Kitty Wells. Kitty, first to hold the unofficial title "Queen of Country Music," was one of the few female country music singers to have a hit record in the 1950s.

By the 1960s, however, there were plenty of hits by female artists, and there were many openings in country music for women. Among the women stars to make a start in that era was Dolly Parton. She came out of the hills of eastern Tennessee to become a nationally known singing star, famous for her high, sweet voice and her glamorous looks.

Only five feet tall, Dolly glides onstage on a typical evening in a luxurious gown or pantsuit, wearing an array of rings and other jewelry. It's a sight that doesn't seem to fit the simple, homespun image of country music, for Dolly looks more like a Hollywood starlet than a Tennessee hill girl. Yet times have changed, and Dolly's glamor represents country music as it is today—big business. Many of today's country song arrangements are more lush and complex than yesterday's simple fiddle pieces. And the awards ceremony that the Country Music Association puts on every year is as elaborate as Hollywood's Academy Awards. Why shouldn't a star's image, then, keep up with the changing times?

Dolly's image is important to her act. She feels that she must maintain her image at all costs in order to please her audience. Once she was late for a meeting with a reporter because she had to put her makeup on. "I never go out in public without it," she says, because people expect her to look like a princess from a fairy tale. "Why," she laughs, "it would shock you to death to see me without my makeup."

Sometimes all that makeup and blond hair get in the way of the real Dolly Parton. She herself realizes this. Told one time that she was a "really beautiful woman," she smiled and said quietly, "Thank you, but I wish you had said 'beautiful person.' There's more to me than looks."

There is, indeed, more to Dolly than just looks. Underneath the makeup and blond wig is a person whom some consider one of the most versatile, intelligent, and talented writer-performers in country music. Dolly writes for other singing stars, but records many of her own compositions herself. Among her many hits are "Muleskinner Blues," "Joshua," "Just Because I'm a Woman," "My Blue Ridge Mountain Boy," "Love is Like a Butterfly," "Jolene," and "Coat of Many Colors." The last song, based on a childhood incident, tells of the time Dolly went to school wearing a coat her mother had sewn together from rags.

Even though some of Dolly's songs are recorded by pop artists and played on pop music stations, she still sees herself as a country performer and writer. A vigorous advocate of country music, she has proudly accepted numerous awards for her singing and songwriting. In 1968, 1970, and 1971, Dolly won the Country Music Association's "Vocal Duo of the Year" award along with Porter Wagoner. And she was named "Female Vocalist of the Year" in 1975 and 1976.

It was just such stardom that Dolly dreamed of when she boarded the bus for Nashville back in 1964. She was only 18 at the time and just out of high school. Dolly was so eager to leave her hometown of Sevierville, Tennessee, that she didn't even take time to do her laundry but carried a bundle of dirty clothes with her. In addition to dirty clothes, Dolly brought a certain measure of determination and talent with her to Nashville.

Dolly's natural musical ability began to develop long before she left for Nashville, however. Avie Lee Parton, her mother, says that Dolly was composing songs even before she could read or write. Dolly got her ideas from the world around her. If nothing caught her fancy, she would draw on her vivid imagination. These childhood songs of

Dolly's wigs and costumes are as much a part of her act as her songs.

Dolly's imagination and heart were always dictated to her mother first.

"I still remember the first time she came and said, 'Mama, I've made a song,'" said Mrs. Parton. "And I still have the first song I wrote down for her." It is, as one might well imagine, a family keepsake.

When Dolly wasn't busy composing songs as a young girl, she was singing. She sang while working around the farm, washing dishes, or taking care of her younger brothers and sisters. And she sang in church. She says the old "shout-em-out" gospel tunes from her girlhood still give her a good feeling today.

Dolly's uncle Bill Owens, a songwriter himself, encouraged Dolly in her singing and writing. When she was 10, he took her to audition for the highly popular Cass Walker television show in Knoxville, Tennessee. Dolly was hired as a regular on the spot, and she remained on the show until she left for Nashville. She also made occasional guest appearances with the "Grand Ole Opry" during her teenage years.

By the time Dolly graduated from high school, she was ready to take Nashville by storm. On her first day there, she met her future husband, Carl Dean. After the two started dating, Carl had to leave for military service. But they were married after he returned in 1966.

Meanwhile, Dolly was having a difficult time with her career. For several months, she lived with her uncle Bill Owens and his wife. He and Dolly pounded the pavement together, trying to sell songs. Her only success in music came when she was hired to record demonstration songs for other songwriters. By that time she was earning just enough money to move into her own apartment, but sometimes she didn't have enough for food. She recalls that the only time she was able to eat well was when she was invited out to dinner.

At long last, Dolly worked herself into a writing contract with Combine Music and a recording contract with Monument Records. Monument did not know quite what to do with her at first. It tried to make Dolly into a rock singer, but her girlish voice just wasn't suitable. Dolly wasn't happy singing rock, either, and she finally persuaded the company to let her "go country." She made a record entitled "Dumb Blond," which became a hit, and followed it up with one of her own compositions, "Something Fishy." That, too, became a hit.

Singer Porter Wagoner then heard about Dolly. For a long time, he had been looking for a woman to sing on his television show, aired in more than 100 cities and seen by millions of people. When Dolly got a call to come to his office, she thought he wanted to talk to her about some songs she had written. Instead, he asked her to audition and soon after offered her the job.

Dolly Parton joined the Wagoner show in the summer of 1967, which was the big break she needed. Soon after, her contract with Monument expired. She then signed with RCA, the company for which Porter recorded. This enabled the two to record duets.

Dolly stayed with Porter until 1974, when they parted on good terms. (The two are still close friends.) Like all talented people, Dolly wanted to strike out on her own, so she put together her own road show. In 1976 she appeared on television in a nationally syndicated program, and she has since hired a new band, Gypsy Fever. She now works out of Hollywood as well as Nashville, and still owns a music publishing company jointly with Porter Wagoner.

Not only has Dolly proven herself in what once was a man's domain—country music—but she has also become a superstar in two very different entertainment worlds—Nashville and Hollywood. Dolly is, indeed, a member of the new breed—she defends the old traditions but she is breaking the way for the new.

Johnny Rodriguez 8

Movies have been based on stories far less dramatic than the real-life success story of Johnny Rodriguez. He is a talented young singer and guitarist who rose from rags to riches with his music—the first Chicano (Mexican-American) to become a nationally known country music star. But before Johnny attained stardom, he was living in a shack with his eight brothers and sisters in Sabinal, Texas, a town about 60 miles west of San Antonio.

Johnny's early life sounds like that of any other young Chicano growing up in Texas. But a turning point for Johnny came when he was 18. A Texas ranger, eager to help young people, steered Johnny into performing. Eventually singer Tom T. Hall heard Rodriguez and invited him to Nashville. There Johnny played with Hall's band and then cut a record of his own, "Pass Me By." Bingo! He was a star!

Johnny's rise to fame, all told, took only two years. Since his first hit record, Rodriguez has had more than 10 hit singles and albums. He has become a favorite on television shows such as "Hee Haw," "Country Music, U.S.A.," "Good Old Nashville Music," and "Midnight Special." And he is even getting some dramatic roles on television and in the movies. Most important of all, he is mobbed by adoring fans nearly every place he goes.

A personable, handsome young man, Rodriguez has what the entertainment industry executives call "charisma"—a special kind of charm. His voice is pure and clear, he has a room-brightening smile and expressive eyes, and his body is trim and athletic. With such personal attractiveness, Johnny Rodriguez is clearly one of country music's newest and biggest stars.

Such stardom was far from Juan Raul Rodriguez's mind when he was growing up in Sabinal. While still a teenager, he worked as a janitor, a ranch hand, and a ditchdigger. In high school, he earned reasonably good grades and played football and basketball. But after graduation, there wasn't much for a Chicano from south Texas to do with his diploma. Johnny ended up spending a lot of time strumming his battered guitar, drinking beer with his friends, and getting in trouble with the law.

Obviously, Johnny was having problems, and Texas Ranger Joaquin Jackson recognized this.

Because of his interest in the welfare of young people, Jackson stepped into Johnny's life and tried to give him some direction. When Jackson heard Johnny sing and strum the guitar, he knew what that direction would be. He introduced young Rodriguez to a friend, James T. Shahan, owner and operator of the Alamo Village Vacationland. Johnny auditioned for Shahan on the stage at Alamo Village. He played "three or four songs," the older man recalled."But I knew after the first line of the first song that he had something."

Shahan hired Johnny to perform in skits, drive a stagecoach, and demonstrate trick shooting for the tourists. He also worked with Johnny on his singing. Along with his other duties, Johnny would sing for the camera-toting tourists at Alamo Village. One day in the fall of 1971, entertainers Tom T. Hall and Bobby Bare stopped in, heard Rodriguez sing, and in a short time were "picking and singing" along with him. That was when Tom T. invited Johnny to Nashville, where Tom promised him a job with his band, the Storytellers. But Nashville seemed a long way off for Rodriguez, who at long last was feeling happy and secure with his life. Although he wasn't saving any money, he did have the jobs with Shahan during the tourist season. And in the off months he found work on the Houston docks or in construction.

Johnny's security was shaken, however, by two

deaths in the Rodriguez family. His father died of cancer in January 1972. Then his brother Andy was killed in an automobile accident. The accident upset Johnny terribly, because Andy was the one who had gotten him started in music. Andy had even given Johnny his old guitar and had taught him how to play and sing, too. Not only that, but the two brothers had always listened to old Merle Haggard, Hank Williams, and Jimmie Rodgers records together.

A few weeks after his brother's death, Johnny picked up his guitar and went to Nashville with eight dollars tucked in his boot. It must have been with some fear that he looked up Tom T. Hall. What if Hall did not remember him? What if he hadn't meant what he said? But Hall did remember Johnny and hired him as the new "front man" in the band, the new lead guitar player. Not only that, but Hall set up an audition for Johnny with Roy Dea of Mercury Records. For the audition, Johnny sang "I Can't Stop Loving You," partly in English, partly in Spanish. Dea was so impressed that before the song was over he decided to sign Johnny.

While establishing a reputation with his own records, Rodriguez was getting a musical education with Hall and the Storytellers. He went on tour with the band and became accustomed to appearing before large crowds. He also had the important experience of performing solo one time before the

"Grand Ole Opry", a surprise planned by Hall. It happened in such a way that Johnny never suspected that he would sing alone that night. A few minutes before the show, Tom T. told him to get a guitar. "You're fixin' to sing," he said. With trembling knees, Johnny went on the Opry stage. He charmed the audience with his singing and even got an encore. He was fast becoming a professional entertainer in his own right.

Rodriguez is now touring on his own. He has moved from Texas to Brentwood, a suburb of Nashville, but he still makes many visits home. During one visit to Sabinal, he went back to one of the first "honky tonk" clubs in which he had worked—a tavern frequented by ranchers and farmhands. "I got five dollars a night and all the beer I could drink," he recalls. "When I went back, everybody looked like they'd seen a ghost. They said, 'God, we never thought you'd come back in here.' It made me feel bad in a way, because people tend to think that you forget. But soon everybody got loose and in the groove." After the ice was broken, it was just like the "good old days," reminisced Johnny.

Young Rodriguez grins everytime he hears the phrase "good old days," for he remembers something that Tom T. Hall once said to him. "Son, most of your good old days are still ahead of you."

Tanya Tucker 9

In the early 1970s, MCA Record executives were looking for a new singer who would appeal to both young people and adults. They wanted somebody who could sing pop (or middle-of-the-road) music, rock, *and* country, so they went after a young lady named Tanya Tucker. She was only 15 at the time and singing for Columbia Records. But MCA executives won her away from Columbia and signed her on her sixteenth birthday—October 10, 1974.

By that time, Tanya had been a recording artist for nearly three years, earning the title of country music's "teen queen" from *Time* magazine. Her music was so good that many country music fans and experts predicted that she would be the future "Queen of Country Music."

But MCA executives hope that Tanya achieves an even greater success than that. They want her to be a superstar of all kinds of music, not just of country music. Ambition toward that goal has helped Tanya change her attitude about rock-and-roll, a kind of music that she once disliked. Now she declares that she likes it—at least some of it. She even sings rock tunes, and some fans compare her rock style to that of Elvis Presley. She sings in a sometimes sultry, sometimes teasing or playful style, just as Presley used to.

Tanya got her real start in country music, just as Presley did. Although her popularity spans all age groups and musical tastes (as MCA had hoped), she is still thought of as a country singer by fans and music industry people. Tanya was one of the five finalists for 1975 Country Music Association "Female Vocalist of the Year" and was named 1976 "Female Country Vocalist of the Year" by *Billboard Magazine*—honors that proclaim Tanya a real country singer.

The fact that Tanya started in country music makes her early success even more remarkable in a way. Ordinarily, good country music requires a sincerity that comes from personal experience. The lyrics generally tell a story with which the performer is familiar. He or she may sing about a personal experience, thus making the song even more heartfelt. The late Hank Williams, a legendary figure in country music, said that in a sad funeral song, for example, the country singer "sees the person lying in the grave." Performers such as

Hank Williams, Johnny Cash, Loretta Lynn, and Merle Haggard all led hard lives. Their hard living gave their songs more color and depth, thus making them more believable.

But Tanya Tucker is the one startling exception to this rule. As a young teenager, she was singing about things she had never known—love, death, and loneliness. How she could sing with such deep feeling about these topics is, of course, a mystery. But like a child prodigy in science or mathematics, Tanya had an advanced understanding of her subject. Not only that, but she also had a naturally beautiful voice with which to tell her story. She had never studied voice in her life, she says, because she didn't need to. "I just opened my mouth and started singing."

Tanya's singing career got under way when she was only eight years old. "I want to be a country singer," she declared to her dad one day. Her father, Beau Tucker, just laughed. But when he started really listening to his daughter, he was amazed at how good she sounded. One time Tanya wanted to sing a Hank Williams' song, "Your Cheating Heart," for him. Beau declared that no little girl, no matter how good, could sing such a soulful tune, but Tanya proved him wrong.

Beau's future as an oil-well rigger was uncertain, and he knew he wanted better things for his daughter. He sensed that there was a special future in store for little Tanya, so he did all he could to give her a start in show business. With Beau's help, Tanya soon got regular work on a local television show in Phoenix, where the Tuckers lived at the time. He even got her into shows and fairs, singing alongside such performers as Mel Tillis, Leroy Van Dyke, and Ernest Tubb. More often than not, the cute little girl with the light hair was able to wangle her own way onto the stage. "I was like a dog with a bone," recalls Tanya of her start in show business. "Nothing could turn me away from performing."

When Tanya was 11, she even got a small part in the movie *Jeremiah Johnson,* starring Robert Redford. The movie was shot in St. George, Utah, where the Tucker family had moved from Phoenix. Another move was soon to come, however, because Beau Tucker had become convinced that his daughter was serious about a career in music. Determined to give her a chance, he quit his job and moved his family to Las Vegas, the nearest city where entertainment was a big business.

Once settled in Las Vegas, Tanya made a demonstration tape of six songs, and Beau started submitting copies to various industry people in Nashville and California. He received rejection after rejection. "She's too young" was always the answer. But there was one person who did not agree. In Las Vegas, a songwriter named Delores Fuller thought that Tanya had definite promise. Through Fuller, a producer from Columbia Records heard about Tanya and invited her to come to Nashville to cut a record.

In March 1972, Fuller, the producer, Tanya, and Beau pored over material for two weeks, looking for a proper song. One evening after a session, Tanya walked into her motel and announced to her family, "We've got it." "It" was "Delta Dawn," a haunting song about a middle-aged woman clinging to the past, wearing a "faded rose from days

Tanya receiving an award for "Most Promising Female Vocalist" in 1976

gone by" and looking for the mysterious dark-haired stranger "who had promised to take her for his bride."

Was the theme appropriate for a 13-year-old? For Tanya Tucker it was. Her astonishingly mature voice, with its power and depth, quickly made the song a number one country hit. Suddenly the entire Tucker family was in show business. Beau bought an old touring bus, painted "Tanya Tucker" on its side, and hired a five-piece band to back Tanya on the road. Tanya's mother, Juanita, was in charge of wardrobe and makeup. Her brother, Don, became her road manager. And her sister, La Costa, also a singer, began pursuing a musical career of her own. (She is now a recording artist for Capitol.)

Following the success of "Delta Dawn," Tanya was booked for as many as 200 nights on the road annually. Regular school, of course, was out of the question at this time, so Tanya turned to tutors and correspondence courses for her education.

But Tanya's real education has been on the stage and behind a recording microphone. In her personal appearances, she sings everything from hard country songs such as "Old Dan Tucker" to sweet pop tunes like "How Can I Tell Him?" She can sing religious tunes like "Why Me, Lord" and patriotic songs—"Dixie" for southern audiences and "Battle Hymn of the Republic" for northern audiences. Her recording career has progressed steadily. There have been hits such as "What's Your Mama's Name?" "Jamestown Ferry," "Would You Lay with Me (In a Field of Stone)," and "The Man Who Turned My Mama On."

Today the Tucker family lives on a 220-acre ranch near Nashville. There, Tanya spends what little spare time she has riding and raising horses. (She named her first horse Delta Dawn—naturally!) She has many pets, including dogs, cats, and deer. The farm provides a comfortable setting, with its rolling pastures, majestic trees, and well-kept lawn.

For someone else, Tanya's farm would be a good place to retire. But for Tanya it is a place to relax and to be with the family between shows and recording sessions. She is a young woman—still the youngest of the new generation of stars. And she says that she hasn't come close to retiring yet. Tanya is going after her goals as she always did—like the "dog with the bone," she will never give up.

Index

Atkins, Chet, 42

barn dances, 5
blind entertainers, 45-46

Campbell, Glen, 9-15
Cash, Johnny, 39
Charles, Ray, 46
classical music, 47
Colter, Jessi, 38, 42
Country Music Association, 34, 37, 46, 52, 53, 66
country music, history of, 5-7, 23-24, 66-67; in the southern United States, 5, 6
country "pop-rock," 10, 17, 34, 39
Crickets (musical group), 41

Dean, Carl, 55
Denver, John, 17-21
Dylan, Bob, 33

Entertainer of the Year award, 14, 17, 37-38
"establishment," the country music, 38-40

Flying Burrito Brothers (musical group), 31
folk singing, 29-30
Ford, Tennessee Ernie, 37

"Glen Campbell Goodtime Hour," 10, 15
"Grand Ole Opry," 37, 49, 63
Gypsy Fever (musical group), 57

Hall, Tom T., 23-27, 59, 61-63
Harris, Emmylou, 29-35
Holly, Buddy, 41-42

Jennings, Waylon, 37-43

Martell, Annie, 20-21
Milsap, Ronnie, 45-49
"musical journalism," Tom T. Hall's music as, 27
Music Row, Nashville's, 40

Nashville (movie), 23
Nashville, Tennessee, 49, 57, 59
Nelson, Willie, 38
Nunely, Billie, 12, 15

Parsons, Gram, 31, 32-33, 34
Parton, Avie Lee, 54-55
Parton, Dolly, 51-57
Peter, Paul, and Mary (musical group), 20-21

Queen of Country Music title, 51, 65

"renegades" of country music, 23
Rodriguez, Johnny, 59-63

Storytellers (musical group), 61, 62

television, the affect of on country music, 6, 9
Tillis, Mel, 37
Tucker, Tanya, 65-71

Wagoner, Porter, 56-57